Ingrid Preedy

Fit fürs Gymnasium
Besser in Englisch
4. Klasse

Die Autorin: Ingrid Preedy ist Englischlehrerin an einer Gesamtschule und Verfasserin zahlreicher Lernhilfen. Sie hat mehrere Jahre an einer Grundschule Englisch unterrichtet.

www.cornelsen.de

Bibliografische Information: Die Deutsche Bibliothek verzeichnet diese Publikation in der Deutschen Nationalbiografie; detaillierte bibliografische Daten sind im Internet über http://dnb.ddb.de abrufbar.

Dieser Band folgt den Regeln der deutschen Rechtschreibung, die seit August 2006 gelten.

6.	5.	4.	3.	2.	Die letzten Ziffern bezeichnen
12	11	10	09	08	Zahl und Jahr der Auflage.

© 2008 Cornelsen Verlag Scriptor GmbH & Co. KG, Berlin
Das Werk und seine Teile sind urheberrechtlich geschützt. Jede Verwertung in anderen als den gesetzlich zugelassenen Fällen bedarf der vorherigen schriftlichen Einwilligung des Verlages.
Hinweis zu den §§ 46, 52 a UrhG: Weder das Werk noch seine Teile dürfen ohne eine solche Einwilligung eingescannt und in ein Netzwerk eingestellt oder sonst öffentlich zugänglich gemacht werden. Dies gilt auch für Intranets von Schulen und sonstigen Bildungseinrichtungen.
Redaktion: Anke Simon, Siegen
Herstellung: Uwe Pahnke, Berlin
Gesamtgestaltung: Dagmar & Torsten Lemme, Berlin
Umschlagentwurf: Bauer & Möhring, Berlin
Illustrationen: Klaus Müller, Berlin
Repro: Heenemann, Berlin
Druck und Bindung: orthdruk, Bialystok, Polen
Printed in Poland
ISBN 978-3-589-22594-1

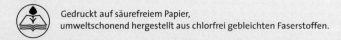
Gedruckt auf säurefreiem Papier,
umweltschonend hergestellt aus chlorfrei gebleichten Faserstoffen.

Inhalt

Vorwort 5

Tipps für das Arbeiten und Lernen 7

Unit 1: Me and my friends 8
    Themen: Körperteile, Aussehen, Farben; *I have got*, Einzahl und Mehrzahl, *is/are*
    A That's me 8
    B My friends 12
    Test: Me and my friends 16

Unit 2: My family 18
    Themen: Familie, Aussehen; *How old are you?*, *he/she has got*, Possessivpronomen *his* und *her*
    A My family 18
    B My friend's family 22
    Test: My family 26

Unit 3: At school 28
    Themen: Schule; Fragen mit *Has he/she got?*, Fragen mit *How many?*, *there is/there are*
    A My schoolbag 28
    B My classroom 32
    Test: At school 36

Unit 4: Hobbies and sports 38
    Themen: Hobbies, Sportarten, Wochentage; Verb *like*, Fragen mit *Do you like?*, Fragen mit *Can you?*
    A My hobbies 38
    B Sports 42
    Test: Hobbies and sports 46

Unit 5: At home 48
    Themen: Zimmer, Einrichtungsgegenstände; unbestimmter Artikel *a/an*, *there is/there are*, Fragen mit *Where is?*, Präpositionen *in*, *on*, *next to*, *under*
    A Rooms 48
    B Sally's house 52
    Test: At home 56

Unit 6: Food and drinks 58
    Themen: Lebensmittel, Getränke; Mehrzahl auf *-es/-ies*, Verb *like*,
    Verb *want*
    A Food 58
    B Drinks 63
    Test: Food and drinks 66

Unit 7: Meals and shopping 68
    Themen: Mahlzeiten, Einkaufen; *always* (immer) und *never* (nie)
    A Meals 68
    B Shopping 73
    Test: Meals and shopping 76

Unit 8: In town 78
    Themen: Fahrzeuge, Gebäude; Beschreibungen mit *I can see*,
    Aufforderungen mit *Let's go*, Verben *want* und *must*
    A In the street 78
    B Places in town 82
    Test: In town 86

Unit 9: Animals 88
    Themen: Tiere; Fragen mit *Where is?*, *there is/there are*, Verb *like*
    A On a farm 88
    B At the zoo 92
    Test: Animals 96

Unit 10: Celebrations 98
    Themen: Weihnachten, Ostern, Halloween, Geburtstag, Monate;
    Präpositionen *in, on, behind, under*, Fragen mit *When?*
    A Seasonal holidays 98
    B My birthday 102
    Test: Celebrations 106

Wörterverzeichnis 108

Vorwort

Liebe Schülerin, lieber Schüler!

Dieses Buch unterstützt dich dabei, den Übergang in das Gymnasium sicher zu meistern. Es gibt dir einen Überblick über die Inhalte, die du für die 5. Klasse wissen musst. Die Themen sind in kleinen, verständlichen Schritten aufbereitet. An vielen Stellen kannst du selbst in das Buch hineinschreiben. Kontrolliere deine Ergebnisse mit dem Lösungsheft.

Mit diesem Buch kannst du auf *zweierlei Weise* arbeiten:

1. **Möglichkeit:** Du fühlst dich insgesamt in Englisch unsicher. Dann arbeite das Buch von vorne bis hinten durch. Nimm dir nicht zu viel auf einmal vor. Bearbeite lieber kleinere Abschnitte, aber dafür regelmäßig, vielleicht sogar täglich.
2. **Möglichkeit:** Du kennst deine Lücken. Du weißt, bei welchen Themen du noch unsicher bist. Dann sieh im Inhaltsverzeichnis nach, picke einzelne Abschnitte heraus und arbeite sie durch.

Und noch einige praktische Tipps zum Lernen mit diesem Buch:
- ▶ Verwende zum Eintragen ins Buch einen Bleistift. Fehler kannst du dann leichter ausbessern.
- ▶ Bist du dir beim Lösen der Übungsaufgaben nicht ganz sicher, lies dir die Beispiele oder Regeln und Tipps noch einmal genau durch.
- ▶ Vergleiche deine Ergebnisse mit dem Lösungsheft.
  Überprüfe bei Fehlern immer genau, was du falsch gemacht hast.
- ▶ Bearbeite die Übungsaufgaben nach einigen Tagen noch einmal.
  So kannst du zusätzliche Sicherheit gewinnen.

Die *Symbole* am Seitenrand bedeuten:

 Wichtige Regel: Präge sie dir genau ein.

 Übungsaufgabe: Löse sie im Buch oder in einem separaten Heft.

 Übung zum Hörverstehen auf der Audio-CD.

 Tipp: Dieser Hinweis hilft dir beim Lernen und Üben.

Vorwort

Liebe Eltern!

Dieses Buch soll Ihrem Kind für das Fach Englisch den Übergang ins Gymnasium erleichtern. Es umfasst die erweiterten Lerninhalte des 4. Schuljahres, wie sie für eine erfolgreiche Arbeit im Fach Englisch in der 5. Klasse des Gymnasiums erforderlich sind. Die einzelnen Lerninhalte werden in zahlreichen Übungen wiederholt und gefestigt. Sie sind so angelegt, dass Ihr Kind die einzelnen Abschnitte selbstständig bearbeiten kann. In der Regel sind dafür täglich etwa 30 Minuten ausreichend.

Und darauf sollten Sie achten:
- Stellen Sie sicher, dass Ihr Kind regelmäßig an den Übungen und Aufgaben arbeitet. Durch zu lange Unterbrechungen wird bereits Gelerntes schnell wieder vergessen.
- Sorgen Sie für eine ruhige Arbeitsatmosphäre und einen geordneten Arbeitsplatz.
- Stellen Sie Ihrem Kind das notwendige Arbeitsmaterial zur Verfügung.
- Sorgen Sie dafür, dass Ihr Kind mit einer entspannten Lernbereitschaft an die Arbeit geht.
- Achten Sie darauf, dass Ihr Kind regelmäßig kurze Pausen macht.
- Freuen Sie sich mit Ihrem Kind über kleine Erfolge und verstärken Sie Erfolgserlebnisse.
- Zeigen Sie Ihrem Kind immer wieder, dass Lernen Spaß macht, weil es das Wissen erweitert und Fähigkeiten stärkt.

Die Autorin

Tipps für das Arbeiten und Lernen

- Richte dir feste Übungszeiten ein.

- Arbeite immer am gleichen Platz, am besten an einem Schreibtisch.

- Achte darauf, dass dein Arbeitsplatz hell und gut gelüftet ist.

- Stelle alle Materialien bereit, die du zum Arbeiten brauchst.

- Entspanne dich, bevor du arbeitest, dann kannst du dich am besten konzentrieren.

- Belohne dich nach dem Arbeiten mit etwas, das du gerne magst (z. B. Spielen, Musik hören).

Und nun viel Spaß und Erfolg!

Unit 1: Me and my friends

A   That's me

Exercise 1

Track 02

a) Hör dir die CD an, zeige auf die Wörter, die du hörst, und sprich sie nach.
b) Verbinde dann die Wörter mit den Bildern.

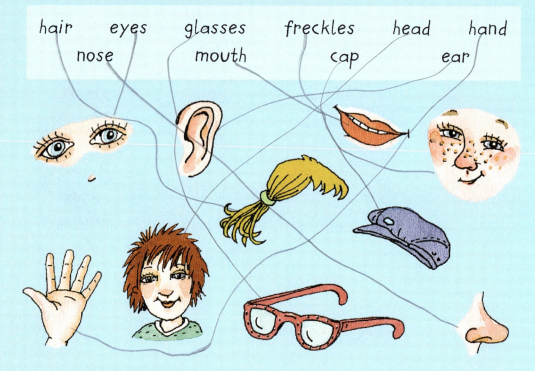

Exercise 2

Track 03

Hör dir die CD an und schreibe die Zahl vor das Wort, das du hörst.

- ⬚1⬚ big
- ⬚6⬚ mouth
- ⬚8⬚ hands
- ⬚4⬚ hair
- ⬚10⬚ head
- ⬚9⬚ glasses
- ⬚5⬚ freckles
- ⬚3⬚ boy
- ⬚2⬚ ears
- ⬚7⬚ girl

Exercise 3

Track 04

a) Wie heißen die Kinder? Hör dir die CD an und schreibe die richtigen Namen unter die Bilder.
b) Lies dann die Sätze unter den Bildern und ergänze die fehlenden Wörter.

Sina | Colin | Tom | Lucie

I have got long fair hair and blue _eyes_.

I have got a little _nose_ with freckles. My hair is red.

I have got short brown _hair_ and brown eyes.

I _have_ got big hands, big _ears_ and a big mouth. I have got red _glasses_.

I have got = ich habe

Exercise 4

Wie lautet das Gegenteil dieser Wörter?

small – _big_
short – _long_

Unit 1: Me and my friends

Einzahl (Singular) und Mehrzahl (Plural)
Im Englischen bildest du die Mehrzahl der meisten Wörter, indem du ein **-s** an das Wort hängst: z. B. ear → ear**s**.

Exercise 5

Einzahl oder Mehrzahl? Schreibe die Wörter in die richtige Spalte.

> head   ears   eyes   nose   boy   hands
> girl   mouth   freckles   cap

Singular (Einzahl)	Plural (Mehrzahl)
head	ears
nose	eyes
boy	hands
girl	freckles
mauth	
cap	

Exercise 6

Wer bin ich? Lies den Text und kreuze die richtige Person an.

Hello, my name is Anna. I am 9 years old. I am small. I have got short brown hair. I have got brown eyes. My nose is small. I have got freckles and glasses. My ears are small and my mouth is small. But my hands are big! Who am I?

Unit 1: Me and my friends

is oder are?
Wenn das Nomen in der Einzahl steht, verwendest du **is**,
z. B. My nose **is** big.
Wenn das Nomen in der Mehrzahl steht, verwendest du **are**,
z. B. My ears **are** small.

Exercise 7

Ergänze die Sätze mit **is** oder **are**.

1. Anna _is_ small.
2. Her eyes _are_ brown.
3. Her nose _is_ small.
4. Her ears _are_ small and her mouth _is_ small.
5. But her hands _are_ big!

Exercise 8

Schreibe nun einige Sätze über dich.

1. My hands _are small._
2. My eyes _are green._
3. My nose _is small._
4. My mouth _is big._

Unit 1: Me and my friends

B My friends

Exercise 1

Track 05

Hör dir die CD an. Wie heißen die Freunde dieser Kinder?

1. Peter's friend is _John_ .
2. Sally's friend is _Anny_ .
3. Tom's friend is _Susan_ .
4. Samantha's friend is _Paul_ .
5. Samuel's friend is _Michael_ .
6. Molly's friend is _Jenny_ .

Unit 1: Me and my friends

Exercise 2

Lies die Sätze. Schau dir die Bilder noch einmal an und trage die Namen ein.

1. This girl has got long brown hair. That's _Susan_.
2. This boy has got red hair and freckles. That's _John_.
3. This girl wears a pink skirt. That's _Jenny_.
4. This boy wears a white T-shirt. That's _Michael_.
5. This girl loves cats. That's _Ann_.
6. This boy has got very short hair. That's _Michael_.
7. This girl wears an orange T-shirt. That's _Jenny_.
8. This boy has got blue eyes and fair hair. That's _Paul_.
9. This girl has got glasses. That's _Susan_.
10. This boy wears green shorts. That's _John_.

Exercise 3

Male die T-Shirts in der richtigen Farbe aus.

Unit 1: Me and my friends

Exercise 4

Male ein Bild von deinem besten Freund oder deiner besten Freundin. Schreibe dann einen Text über ihn/sie.

My best friend

My friend is Nicolas.
My friend has got short and fair hair.
My friend wears a green T-Shirt.
My friend loves football.

Tipp: So kannst du deine Sätze beginnen:
My friend is ... (Mein Freund/meine Freundin ist ...)
My friend has got ... (Mein Freund/meine Freundin hat ...)
My friend wears ... (Mein Freund/meine Freundin trägt ...)
My friend loves ... (Mein Freund/meine Freundin liebt ...)

14 Unit 1: Me and my friends

Exercise 5

In diesem Quadrat haben sich 10 Wörter versteckt. Kreise sie ein und schreibe sie dann auf die Zeilen unten.

N	T	B	P	M	O	U	T	H	M
H	Q	N	O	S	E	Q	G	H	V
V	P	H	A	I	R	Z	X	F	S
Z	G	N	C	H	A	N	D	S	Z
R	A	O	C	C	U	H	E	A	D
H	G	L	A	S	S	E	S	B	H
J	H	Y	Z	K	H	E	E	Q	K
K	F	R	E	C	K	L	E	S	S
E	A	R	S	C	A	P	R	I	Q
F	E	P	C	L	E	Y	E	S	X

Freckles   Mouth
Glasses   Nose
Eyes   Ears
Hair   Hands
Head   Cap

Unit 1: Me and my friends

Test: Me and my friends

Exercise 1

Wie heißen diese Körperteile auf Englisch?

_____   _____   _____   _____

_____   _____   _____   _____

Exercise 2

Finde die fehlenden Buchstaben.

1. My b e st fr i e nd i s a b o y.
2. H e 's n a me i s Colin.
3. H e is 9 years o ld.
4. H e is v e ry b i g.
5. H e h a s g o t bl a ck h a i r.
6. H e h a s g o t fr e ckl e s and a v e ry sm a ll n o s e .

16   Unit 1: Me and my friends

Exercise 3

Track 06

a) Wer ist Bob? Hör dir die CD an und kreuze die richtige Person an.

b) Was sagt Bob über sich? Schreibe 3 Sätze.

_____

_____

_____

Exercise 4

Track 07

Lies das Gedicht und hör es dir auf der CD an. Versuche, es auswendig zu lernen.

This is me

This is me, from my head to my toes.
I have got two brown eyes and a very big nose.
I can wiggle my ears and stamp my feet.
From my head to my toes, I'm really sweet!

toes

feet

Tipp: Am Ende des Buches gibt es ein Wörterverzeichnis. Dort kannst du z. B. nachschlagen, was die Verben wiggle und stamp bedeuten. Versuche aber erst einmal, die Bedeutung selbst zu erraten!

Unit 1: Me and my friends

Unit 2: My family

A My family

Exercise 1

Track 08
a) Hör dir die CD an und zeige auf die Wörter, die du hörst.
b) Hör dir die CD dann noch einmal an und verbinde die Wörter mit den Bildern.

Exercise 2

Schau dir die Bilder noch einmal an und lies die Sätze. Finde heraus, wer gemeint ist.

1. This person is a boy. He has got long brown hair.

   That's Tom's _____.

2. This person has got glasses and big ears.

   That's Tom's _____.

3. This person has got short dark brown hair.

   That's Tom's _____.

4. This person has got long white hair.

   That's Tom's _____.

5. This person has got long dark brown hair.

   That's Tom's _____.

6. This person has got fair hair and glasses.

   That's Tom's _____.

7. This person has got short red hair and freckles.

   That's _____.

8. This person has got a purple T-shirt.

   That's Tom's _____.

9. This person has got a green T-shirt.

   That's Tom's _____.

10. This person has got brown hair and a blue T-shirt.

    That's Tom's _____.

Erinnerst du dich?
he/she has got = er/sie hat
z. B. **She has got** red hair. Sie hat rote Haare.

Unit 2: My family

Exercise 3

Verbinde die Wörter mit den Zahlen.

9	twelve
12	forty-five
14	nine
41	seventy
45	fourteen
70	seventy-five
75	forty-one

Exercise 4

Track 09

Hör dir noch einmal die CD an. Lies die Sätze und schreibe auf, wer gemeint ist.

1. This person is 9 years old. That is _Tom_____.
2. This person is 45. That is Tom's _____.
3. This person is 41. That is Tom's _____.
4. This person is 12 years old. That is Tom's _____.
5. This person is 70. That is Tom's _____.
6. This person is 75. That is Tom's _____.
7. This person is 14 years old. That is Tom's _____.

Tipp: Die Personen werden auf der CD in einer anderen Reihenfolge genannt. Hör dir die Sätze, wenn nötig, mehrmals an.

Unit 2: My family

Exercise 5

Wie alt sind sie? Ergänze die Sätze.

1. How old is Tom?

   Tom is _____ years old.

2. How old is Tom's sister?

   Tom's sister is _____ years old.

3. How old is Tom's mother?

   Tom's _____ .

4. How old is Tom's grandmother?

   _____ .

5. How old is Tom's father?

   _____ .

6. How old is Tom's brother?

   _____ .

7. How old is Tom's grandfather?

   _____ .

Exercise 6

How old are you?

I am _____ years old.

Exercise 7

Wie alt sind die Mitglieder deiner Familie?

My _____ is _____ years old.

My _____ is _____ years old.

_____

_____

_____

Unit 2: My family

B My friend's family

Exercise 1

Track 10

Familie Black, White oder Green? Hör dir die CD an und schreibe die Namen der Familien unter die Bilder.

_____

_____

_____

his und **her**

his = sein, seine   z. B. **His** nose is big. = Seine Nase ist groß.
her = ihr, ihre   z. B. **Her** hands are small. = Ihre Hände sind klein.

Unit 2: My family

Exercise 2

Track 11

a) Hör dir noch einmal die CD an. Wie alt sind Jack und seine Geschwister?

Jack is _____ years old.

His sister is _____ years old.

His brother is _____ years old.

b) Sieh dir nun das Bild an und ergänze die Sätze.

This is my friend, Jack. Jack is _____ years old.

His sister is _____.

She has got _____.

His brother is _____.

He has got _____.

_____ father has got _____.

_____ mother has got _____.

Tipp: Bei dieser Übung kannst du über das Alter und das Aussehen der Personen schreiben.

Exercise 3

Track 12

a) Hör dir noch einmal die CD an. Wie alt sind Jennifer und ihre Geschwister?

Jennifer is _____ years old.

Her sister is _____ years old.

Her brother is _____ years old.

b) Sieh dir nun das Bild an und ergänze die Sätze.

This is my friend, Jennifer. Jennifer is _____ years old.

Her sister is _____.

_____.

_____.

_____.

_____.

Exercise 4

Track 13

a) Hör dir die CD an und lies, was Jack über seinen Familienstammbaum sagt.

This is Tim, my brother.   This is Mia, my sister.
This is David, my father.   This is Paula, my mother.
This is Herbert, my grandfather. This is Betty, my grandmother.
This is Peter, my uncle.   This is Jane, my aunt.
This is Tony, my cousin.   This is Ann, my cousin.

Unit 2: My family

b) Trage diese Wörter in den Stammbaum ein.

> sister   mother   grandfather   aunt (2x)
> cousin (2x)   brother   grandmother   father   uncle

Betty   Herbert

Mary   Peter   Jane   David   Paula

Tony   Ann   Jack   Tim   Mia

Unit 2: My family

Test: My family

Exercise 1

Brown, White oder Green, wie heißt diese Familie?

1. Hi, my name is Linda Brown. I'm eight years old. I have got two brothers, Tim and Bob. Tim is twelve and Bob is fourteen. We live with my mother and my grandfather and grandmother. We have got a little dog. His name is Linus.

2. My name is Colin White. I have got one brother and one sister. Their names are Susan and Peter. Susan is sixteen and Peter is three. My father is forty-three and my mother is forty-one. We have got a big dog. His name is Gus. He's old. He's nine years old. I'm nine years old, too.

3. I'm Gordon Green. I have got one sister, Tracy. She is eleven. I'm only eight. We live with my mother and my grandfather and grandmother. We have got a little cat. Her name is Sammy.

Exercise 2

Ergänze die fehlenden Vokale.

1. M ___ TH ___ R
2. ___ NCL ___
3. ___ ___ NT
4. S ___ ST ___ R
5. GR ___ NDM ___ TH ___ R
6. BR ___ TH ___ R
7. F ___ TH ___ R
8. GR ___ NDF ___ TH ___ R

Wie viele Vokale hast du gebraucht?

Unit 2: My family

Exercise 3

Löse dieses Familienkreuzworträtsel. Trage alle Begriffe in Englisch ein.

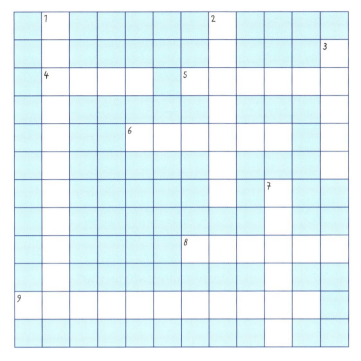

Across →:
4 Tante   **5** Cousin/Cousine   **6** Vater   **8** Schwester   **9** Großmutter

Down ↓:
1 Großvater   **2** Bruder   **3** Onkel   **7** Mutter

Exercise 4

Track 14

Hör dir dieses Gedicht auf der CD an. Versuche, es auswendig zu lernen.

My family

My mother's name is Ann.
My sister's name is Sue.
My father is my uncle's brother
And he is thirty-two.

Unit 3: At school

A My schoolbag

Exercise 1

Track 15

Hör dir die CD an und zeige auf die Dinge. Schreibe dann die richtige Zahl vor jedes Wort.

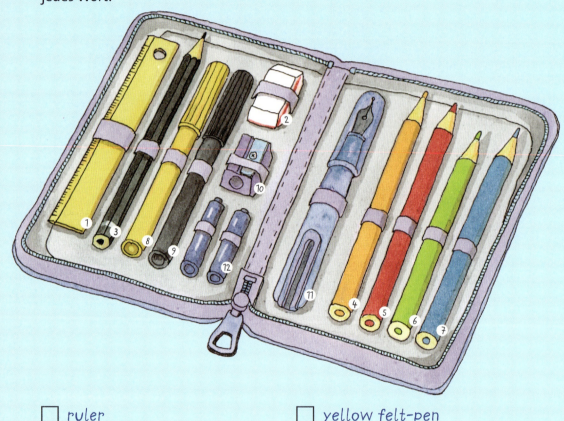

- ☐ ruler
- ☐ red pencil
- ☐ ink cartridge
- ☐ green pencil
- ☐ pencil sharpener
- ☐ orange pencil
- ☐ yellow felt-pen
- ☐ black pencil
- ☐ blue pencil
- ☐ rubber
- ☐ black felt-pen
- ☐ pen

Exercise 2

Was gehört Tom, was gehört Betty? Folge den Linien und trage dann die Sachen in die richtige Spalte ein.

Tom's things	Betty's things
ruler	

Fragen mit Has he/she got?
Fragen mit Has he/she got? beantwortest du mit Yes, he/she has. oder No, he/she hasn't.

Exercise 3

a) Beantworte die Fragen wie in den Beispielen.

Has Tom got a ruler?	Yes, he has.
Has Betty got a rubber?	Yes, she has.
Has Tom got a rubber?	No, he hasn't.
Has Betty got a ruler?	No, she hasn't.

1. Has Tom got a green pencil? _____
2. Has Betty got a pencil sharpener? _____
3. Has Tom got a red pen? _____
4. Has Tom got a red pencil? _____
5. Has Betty got a red felt-pen? _____
6. Has Betty got an orange pencil? _____
7. Has Betty got an ink cartridge? _____
8. Has Tom got a blue pen? _____
9. Has Tom got a blue pencil? _____
10. Has Betty got a black pencil? _____

b) Schreibe Sätze.

1. Tom has got a ruler _____.
2. Betty has got _____.
3. _____.
4. _____.

Unit 3: At school

Exercise 4

a) Schau dir Johns Tasche an und verbinde alle Wörter, die du schon kennst, mit dem richtigen Gegenstand.

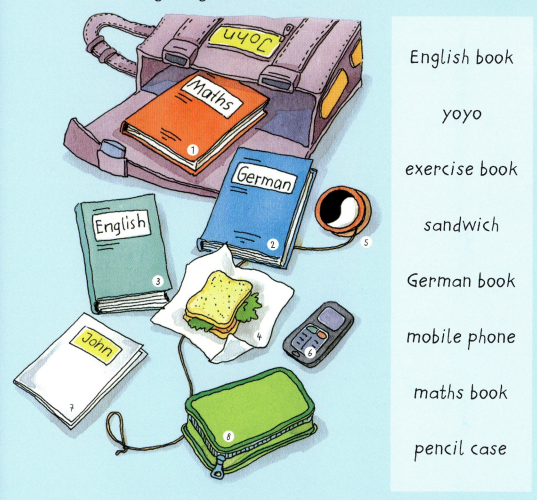

b) Hör dir jetzt die CD an und verbinde alle neuen Wörter mit den Bildern.
c) Lies und ergänze diese Sätze.

1. It is white. That is John's _exercise book_____.
2. It is black. That is John's _____.
3. It is green. That is John's _____.
4. It is red. That is John's _____.
5. It is blue. That is John's _____.
6. It is black and white. That is John's _____.

Unit 3: At school

B My classroom

Exercise 1
Schau dir das Klassenzimmer der 4 A an. Lies dann die Wörter und unterstreiche alle, die du schon kennst.

Class 4 A's classroom

window   door   teacher   chalk   duster   sponge

board   map   CD-player   bookshelf   chair   table

Exercise 2

Track 17

Hör dir die CD an und ergänze zum Bild auf S. 32.

1. _teacher_   7. _____
2. _____   8. _____
3. _____   8. _____
4. _____   10. _____
5. _____   11. _____
6. _____   12. _____

Exercise 3

Schau dir noch einmal das Bild auf S. 32 an und beantworte die Fragen.

1. How many tables are there? There are _5_ tables.
2. How many chairs are there? There are _____ chairs.
3. How many windows are there? There are _____ windows.
4. How many maps are there? There are _____ maps.
5. How many teachers are there? There is _____ teacher.
6. How many CD-players are there? There is _____ CD-player.

Fragen mit How many?
Fragen mit How many? (Wie viele?) beantwortest du mit:
There is ..., wenn es nur eins der in der Frage genannten Dinge gibt, z. B.
There **is** one board.
There are ..., wenn es mehrere der in der Frage genannten Dinge gibt, z. B.
There **are** three chairs.

Unit 3: At school

Exercise 4

Track 18

a) Hör dir die CD an. Wie viele dieser Dinge (und Personen) befinden sich in Susans Klassenzimmer?

tables: __6__ bookshelves: _____

chairs: _____ sponges: _____

windows: _____ boards: _____

computers: _____ doors: _____

CD-players: _____ teachers: _____

b) Ergänze nun die Sätze.

1. There _are 6 tables_ in Susan's classroom.
2. There are _____ chairs.
3. There _____ _____ windows.
4. There _____ _____ computers.
5. There _____ _____ _____ .
6. There _____ _____ _____ .
7. There is _____ board.
8. There _____ _____ door.
9. There _____ _____ _____ .
10. There _____ _____ _____ .

Exercise 5

Ordne alle passenden Wörter in die beiden Kategorien auf S. 35 oben ein. Wörter, die nichts mit Schule zu tun haben, brauchst du nicht zu schreiben.

legrulerchairmotherpencilsharpenerrubberbrotherbook
peninkcartridgeCD-playersisterbookshelfbrown
exercisebooktablefelt-penwindowdoor
teacherfatherchalkmouthpencilcasedustersponge

Unit 3: At school

Exercise 6

Bilde Sätze.

1. classroom / small / is / My
_____

2. Today / are / five / boys / and / one / teacher / there
_____

3. We / one / got / computer / have
_____

4. There / one chair / for the boys / is / five chairs / are / for the teacher / there / and
_____
_____

Test: At school

Exercise 1

Track 19

Hör dir an, was Linda sagt und male die Gegenstände in der richtigen Farbe aus.

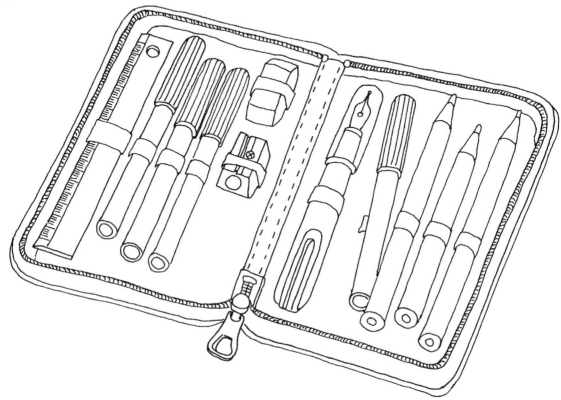

Exercise 2

Ergänze die Wörter.

1. SP _ _ _ _
2. WIN _ _ _
3. DO _ _
4. DUS _ _ _
5. BO _ _ _
6. TAB _ _

7. TEA _ _ _ _
8. CH _ _ K
9. CH _ _ R
10. M _ _
11. BOOK _ _ _ _ _
12. PEN _ _ _

Unit 3: At school

Exercise 3

Löse dieses Kreuzworträtsel zum Thema Schule.
Trage alle Begriffe auf Englisch ein.

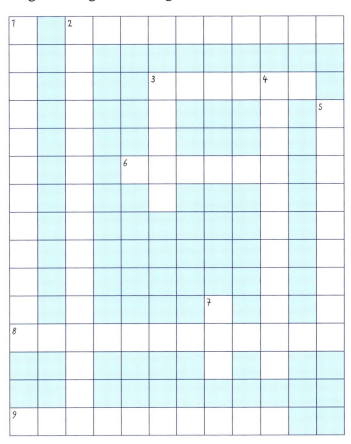

Across →:
2 Etui   3 Radiergummi   6 Bleistift   8 Heft   9 Deutschbuch

Down ↓:
1 Tintenpatrone   2 Bleistiftspitzer   3 Lineal   4 Englischbuch
5 Mathebuch   7 Füller

Unit 4: Hobbies and sports

A My hobbies

Exercise 1

Betty hat sehr viele Hobbys. Lies den Text und schreibe den richtigen Wochentag unter jedes Bild.

Betty's week
On Monday Betty goes to ballet.
On Tuesday Betty goes swimming.
On Wednesday Betty goes horse riding.
On Thursday Betty listens to music.
On Friday Betty plays tennis.
On Saturday Betty watches football on TV.
On Sunday Betty plays chess with her grandmother.

_____ _____ _____ _____

_____ _____ _____

 Die Wochentage werden im Englischen immer großgeschrieben!

Exercise 2

Ergänze die fehlenden Buchstaben.

M ___ ND ___ Y   F ___ ID ___ ___

T ___ ___ S ___ A ___   S ___ ___ ___ RDA ___

W E ___ ___ E ___ DAY   SU ___ D ___ Y

T ___ ___ RSD ___ Y

Exercise 3

Track 20

Diese Woche ist alles anders als sonst! Hör dir die CD an und ergänze Bettys Terminkalender.

ballet

chess

horse riding

Monday
Tuesday
Wednesday
Thursday
Friday
Saturday
Sunday

tennis

music

swimming

football on TV

Unit 4: Hobbies and sports

Exercise 4

Track 21

a) Welche Spiele mögen diese Kinder? Hör dir die CD an und verbinde die Namen mit dem richtigen Spiel.

Michael		chess
Susan		Monopoly
Gordon		cards
Mia		dominoes
Lara		Bingo
David		Trivial Pursuit
Sandra		Snakes and Ladders

Tipp: Wenn du das Spiel Snakes and Ladders nicht kennst, kannst du es dir auf S. 74 anschauen!

b) Ergänze nun die Sätze.

1. Michael likes playing _____.
2. Susan likes playing _____.
3. Gordon likes _____ _____.
4. David likes _____ _____.
5. Lara _____ _____ _____.
6. Sandra _____ _____ _____.
7. Mia _____ _____ _____.

Das Verb like
I like = ich mag
he/she likes = er/sie mag
An das Verb like kannst du ein Nomen oder ein weiteres Verb in der ing-Form anschließen, z. B.: I **like** football. Ich mag Fußball.
She **likes** play**ing** cards. Sie spielt gerne Karten.

Unit 4: Hobbies and sports

Exercise 5

Welche Spiele magst du? Schreibe drei Sätze.

1. I like playing _____.
2. I like _____ _____.
3. I like _____ _____.

> **Fragen mit Do you like …?**
> Auf die Frage Do you like …? (Magst du …?) antwortest du mit Yes, I do. oder No, I don't.

Exercise 6

Beantworte die Fragen.

1. Do you like playing Monopoly? _Yes, I do._ _____
2. Do you like playing Trivial Pursuit? _No, I don't._ _____
3. Do you like playing chess? _____
4. Do you like playing card games? _____
5. Do you like playing Bingo? _____
6. Do you like horse riding? _____
7. Do you like football? _____

Exercise 7

Denke dir nun drei Fragen mit Do you like …? aus, die du einem englischen Kind stellen könntest.

1. Do you like _____?
2. _____?
3. _____?

Unit 4: Hobbies and sports

B Sports

Exercise 1

Track 22

a) Schreibe alle Sportarten, die du kennst, unter die Bilder.
b) Hör dir dann die CD an, überprüfe deine Antworten und ergänze die fehlenden Begriffe.

> judo   swimming   inline skating   table tennis
> cycling   ice skating   basketball
> horse riding   hockey   tennis

_____   _____   _____   _____   _____

_____   _____   _____   _____   _____

Exercise 2

Kannst du erraten, welche Sportarten diese Kinder mögen?

1. Tom likes NISNET and ENLINI GINTKAS. _tennis_ and _____
2. Jane likes DOJU and BELAT NISNET. _____ and _____
3. Jenny likes NIGLYCC and SKALLBBTEA. _____ and _____
4. Amy likes EINNST and CIE NIGTASK. _____ and _____
5. Paul likes KEYOCH. _____
6. Mary likes NIGWIMMS and SHORE NIGDIR. _____ and _____

Unit 4: Hobbies and sports

Exercise 3

Track 23

a) Was können diese Kinder spielen? Hör dir die CD an und kreuze das richtige Kästchen an. Aufgepasst: Jedes Kind kann immer nur **eins** der drei Dinge spielen.

1. Jane can play ☐ football ☐ basketball ☐ table tennis
2. Peter can play ☐ the guitar ☐ football ☐ cards
3. Carol can play ☐ tennis ☐ table tennis ☐ football
4. Tim can play ☐ basketball ☐ football ☐ hockey
5. Robert can play ☐ tennis ☐ hockey ☐ basketball
6. Hannah can play ☐ chess ☐ hockey ☐ the guitar

I can = ich kann
I can't = ich kann nicht

---

b) Beantworte nun die Fragen. Die Farbe hinter der richtigen Antwort gibt an, in welcher Farbe du das entsprechende Feld des Mandalas ausmalen sollst. Beispiel:

1. Can Jane play football?
   ☒ Yes, she can. (blue)   ☐ No, she can't. (red)

   Die richtige Antwort ist: *Yes, she can.*
   Du malst also alle Teile mit der Nummer 1 blau aus.

2. Can Hannah play chess?
   ☐ Yes, she can. (yellow)   ☐ No, she can't. (red)
3. Can Carol play football?
   ☐ Yes, she can. (blue)   ☐ No, she can't. (yellow)
4. Can Tim play basketball?
   ☐ Yes, he can. (blue)   ☐ No, he can't. (green)
5. Can Peter play football?
   ☐ Yes, he can. (blue)   ☐ No, he can't. (brown)
6. Can Carol play tennis?
   ☐ Yes, she can. (blue)   ☐ No, she can't. (white)
7. Can Peter play the guitar?
   ☐ Yes, he can. (black)   ☐ No, he can't. (red)
8. Can Robert play hockey?
   ☐ Yes, he can. (pink)   ☐ No, he can't. (red)
9. Can Jane play table tennis?
   ☐ Yes, she can. (blue)   ☐ No, she can't. (orange)
10. Can Tim play football?
    ☐ Yes, he can. (blue)   ☐ No, he can't. (purple)

Unit 4: Hobbies and sports

 Fragen mit Can you ...?
Auf die Frage Can you ...? (Kannst du ...?) antwortest du mit Yes, I can. oder No, I can't.

 ## Exercise 4

a) Was kannst du spielen? Beantworte die Fragen mit Yes, I can. oder No, I can't.

1. Can you play tennis? _____

2. Can you play basketball? _____

3. Can you play football? _____

4. Can you play table tennis? _____

b) Schreibe nun ganze Sätze.

I can play _____.

_____.

I can't play _____.

_____.

Unit 4: Hobbies and sports

Exercise 5

Bilde Sätze.

1. I / play / can / the guitar _____
2. hockey / Robert / play / can _____
3. table tennis / play / I / can't _____

Exercise 6

Schreibe die Sportarten in die richtige Tabellenspalte. Manche Sportarten kannst du in mehrere Spalten eintragen.

basketball   cycling   hockey   horse riding
ice skating   inline skating   judo   swimming
table tennis   tennis

one person	two people	a team	outside (draußen)	inside (drinnen)

Test: Hobbies and sports

Exercise 1

Track 24

a) Schau dir Mikes Kalender an und ergänze die fehlenden Wochentage.
b) Hör dir nun die CD an und vervollständige Mikes Terminkalender.

Exercise 2

Wie heißen Bettys Hobbys auf Englisch?

Unit 4: Hobbies and sports

Exercise 3

Löse dieses Kreuzworträtsel zum Thema Hobbys und Sport. Trage alle Begriffe auf Englisch ein.

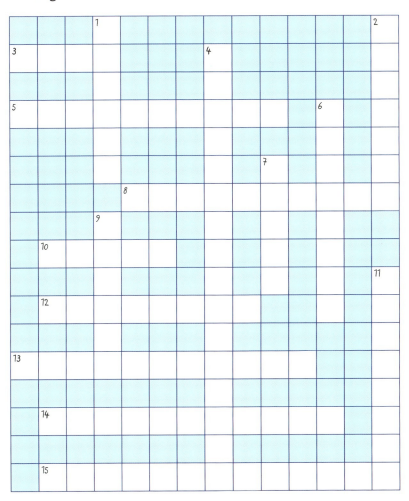

Across →:
3 Judo   5 Basketball   8 Schlittschuhlaufen   10 Schach
12 Brettspiel, bei dem man Straßen und Gebäude kauft   13 Reiten
14 Tischtennis   15 Inlineskating

Down ↓:
1 Hockey   2 Radfahren   4 Brettspiel, bei dem man Leitern herauf- und Schlangen hinuntergeht   6 Domino   7 Karten   9 Tennis   11 Schwimmen

Unit 5: At home

A Rooms

Exercise 1

Track 25

a) Schau dir Johns Zimmer an und lies die Wörter in dem Kasten. Schreibe auf S. 49 alle Wörter auf, die du schon kennst.

> bed   pullover   football   cage   bookshelf   lamp
> bedside table   carpet   aquarium   wardrobe   table
> blanket   computer   books   hamster   goldfish
> shoes   computer mouse   alarm clock   tennis racket

 Tipp: Einige dieser Wörter sind auf Englisch und Deutsch sehr ähnlich. Du kannst also ihre Bedeutung erraten, auch wenn du das englische Wort vorher noch nicht kanntest.

b) Hör dir nun die CD an und ergänze die noch fehlenden Wörter.

48   Unit 5: At home

1. *bed* _____   11. _____
2. _____   12. _____
3. _____   13. _____
4. _____   14. _____
5. _____   15. _____
6. _____   16. _____
7. _____   17. _____
8. _____   18. _____
9. _____   19. _____
10. _____   20. _____

> **a oder an?**
> Erinnerst du dich?
> **an** schreibst du vor Vokalen, also a, e, i, o, u, z. B. **an orange book**
> **a** schreibst du vor Konsonanten, z. B. **a football**

Exercise 2

Schreibe **a** oder **an** vor diese Wörter.

1. __*a*__ bed   5. _____ orange blanket
2. _____ alarm clock   6. _____ bedside table
3. _____ bookshelf   7. _____ computer
4. _____ old lamp   8. _____ aquarium

Exercise 3

Errate die Wörter.

1. EDB _____   5. RAAUIUQM _____
2. LABLOFOT _____   6. SKOLBOHEF _____
3. OBOKS _____   7. SMEUO _____
4. STERMHA _____   8. PMLA _____

Exercise 4

Schau dir noch einmal das Bild auf S. 48 an. Wo sind Johns Sachen? Setze die richtige Präposition ein.

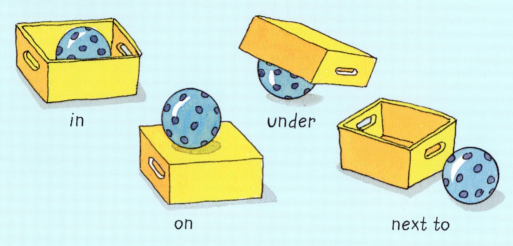

1. There is a bedside table _____ the bed.
2. There are shoes _____ the bed.
3. There are books _____ the aquarium.
4. There is a teddy bear _____ the orange blanket.
5. There is a goldfish _____ the aquarium.
6. There is a computer _____ the table.
7. There is an alarm clock _____ the bookshelf.

Weißt du noch, wann du there is und wann there are schreiben musst? Wenn nicht, dann schau auf S. 33 nach!

Exercise 5

Setze There is oder There are ein.

1. _____ a teddy bear in the bed.
2. _____ books on the bookshelf.
3. _____ a hamster in the cage.
4. _____ shoes next to the bed.

Unit 5: At home

Exercise 6

Zeichne hier dein Zimmer (oder einen Teil davon) und schreibe dann fünf Sätze.

1. There is _____ .
2. There are _____ .
3. _____ .
4. _____ .
5. _____ .

Unit 5: At home

B Sally's house

Exercise 1

Track 26

a) Was macht Sally wo? Verbinde jedes Bild mit dem passenden Satz.
b) Hör dir nun die CD an und ergänze deine Lösungen.

1

Sally is in the attic. She is looking for her father's old tennis racket.

Sally is in her bedroom. She is getting up.

Sally is helping her mother in the kitchen.

Sally is in the bathroom. She is washing herself.

Sally is in the hall. She is putting on her jacket.

Sally is doing her homework in the dining room.

Sally is in the kitchen. She is having breakfast.

Sally is watching TV in the living room.

5

6

2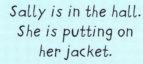

3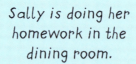

7

4

8

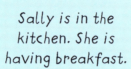

52   Unit 5: At home

Exercise 2

Beantworte die Fragen.

1. Where is Sally washing herself? <u>In the bathroom.</u>
2. Where is Sally doing her homework? _____ .
3. Where is Sally having breakfast? _____ .
4. Where is Sally watching TV? _____ .
5. Where is Sally putting on her jacket? _____ .
6. Where is Sally helping her mother? _____ .
7. Where is Sally looking for her father's old tennis racket?

   _____ .

Exercise 3

Track 27

Colin macht alles ein bisschen anders als Sally. Hör dir die CD an und kreuze die richtige Antwort an.

1. Where is Colin washing himself?
   ☐ In the bathroom.   ☐ In the kitchen.   ☐ In the attic.
2. Where is Colin doing his homework?
   ☐ In the kitchen.   ☐ In the bedroom.   ☐ In the living room.
3. Where is Colin having breakfast?
   ☐ In the bathroom.   ☐ In the dining room.   ☐ In the kitchen.
4. Where is Colin watching TV?
   ☐ In the living room.   ☐ In the bedroom.   ☐ In the hall.
5. Where is Colin putting on his jacket?
   ☐ In the bedroom.   ☐ In the living room.   ☐ In the hall.
6. Where is Colin helping his mother?
   ☐ In the dining room.   ☐ In the kitchen.   ☐ In the attic.
7. Where is Colin looking for his old teddy bear?
   ☐ In the kitchen.   ☐ In the attic.   ☐ In the bedroom.

Unit 5: At home

Exercise 4

Trenne die Wörter mit einem Bleistift. Trage sie dann in die richtige Tabellenspalte ein.

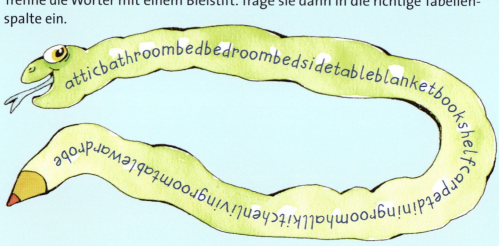

Zimmer	Einrichtungsgegenstände

Exercise 5

Bilde Sätze.

1. in / a new / the / living / TV / room / there / is

    There _____.

2. is / the kitchen / a / in / chair / there

    There _____.

3. chairs / four / are / there / room / dining / the / in

    There _____.

Unit 5: At home

Exercise 6

a) Zeichne einen Plan von deinem Haus oder deiner Wohnung und trage alle Zimmer ein.

b) Vervollständige nun die Sätze.

I have breakfast in the _____ .

I wash my hands in the _____ .

I do my homework in the _____ .

I watch TV in the _____ .

I put on my jacket in the _____ .

Unit 5: At home

Test: At home

Exercise 1

Track 28

a) Hör dir die CD an und male die genannten Gegenstände in den richtigen Farben aus.

Jennifer's room

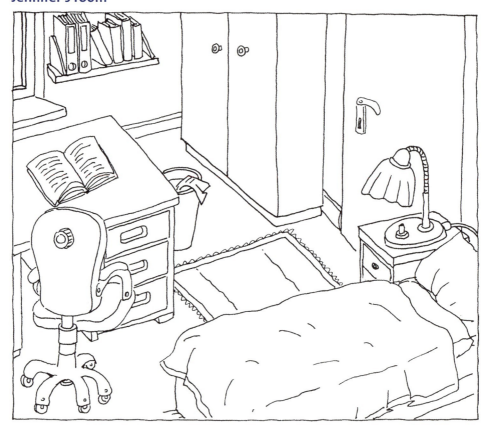

b) Hör dir nun die CD noch einmal an und vervollständige den Text.

This is Jennifer's room. Her _____ is red. On the bed there

is a blanket. The _____ is orange. Next to the bed there is

a _____. The carpet is yellow and blue. The bedside table is white.

There is a _____ on the table. It is red. The bookshelf is brown.

Jennifer's _____ is blue and her table is blue, too.

The _____ is pink.

Unit 5: At home

Exercise 2

Lies die Sätze und trage die richtigen Zimmer ins Kreuzworträtsel ein.

Across →:
1 Sally is putting on her jacket here.
5 Sally is helping her mother here.
6 Sally is watching TV here.
7 Sally is sleeping here.

Down ↓:
2 Sally is looking for a tennis racket here.
3 Sally is doing her homework here.
4 Sally is washing her hands here.

Unit 6: Food and drinks

A Food

Exercise 1

Tracks 29/30

a) Hör dir die CD an und verbinde die Wörter mit den richtigen Obst- und Gemüsesorten.
b) Hör dir die CD dann noch einmal an und sprich die Sätze nach.

bananas   oranges   plums   strawberries   cherries
apples   peaches   grapes   kiwis   melons

potatoes   peas   onions   carrots

Exercise 2

Was ist in diesen Einkaufskörben?

_____   _____   _____
_____   _____   _____
_____   _____   _____
_____   _____   _____
                 _____

Exercise 3

Welche Farben haben die verschiedenen Obst- und Gemüsesorten in den Körben?

The bananas are *yellow* .

The cherries are _____ .

The kiwis are _____ .

The carrots are _____ .

The peas are _____ .

The potatoes are _____ .

Tipp: Wenn du dir nicht mehr sicher bist, wie man die Farben schreibt, dann schau auf S. 13 oder im Wörterverzeichnis nach!

Exercise 4

Löse das Rätsel.

1.
2.
3.
4.
5.
6.
7.
8.

Lösungswort: _____

Unit 6: Food and drinks

> **Die Mehrzahl (Plural)**
> Erinnerst du dich? Du bildest die Mehrzahl der meisten englischen Wörter, in dem du ein **-s** an das Wort hängst.
> Beispiel:
> one pea → two peas
>
> Bei Wörtern, die auf **-ch**, **-s**, **-sh**, **-x**, **-o** enden, wird **-es** an das Wort gehängt.
> Beispiel:
> one tomato → two tomatoes
>
> Bei Wörtern, die auf **-y** enden, fällt in der Mehrzahl das **y** weg und wird durch **-ies** ersetzt.
> Beispiel:
> one cherry → two cherries

Exercise 5

Schreibe die Wörter in der Mehrzahl.

1. one apple — two *apples*
2. one banana — two ___
3. one potato — two ___
4. one tomato — two ___
5. one cherry — two ___
6. one strawberry — two ___
7. one peach — two ___
8. one kiwi — two ___
9. one pea — two ___
10. one carrot — two ___

Unit 6: Food and drinks

Exercise 6

Track 31

a) Hör dir die CD an und kreuze an, was die Kinder mögen.

b) Ergänze nun die Sätze.

1. Peter likes _____ . He doesn't like cherries.

2. Mark likes _____ . He doesn't like _____ .

3. Janet likes _____ . She doesn't like _____ .

4. Sally _____ _____ .

   She _____ _____ _____ .

5. Diana _____ _____ .

   She _____ _____ _____ .

And you?

I like _____ . I don't like _____ .

Unit 6: Food and drinks

B Drinks

Exercise 1
Schau dir die Getränkekarte an und ergänze die fehlenden Wörter.

Exercise 2

Track 32

a) Was wollen die Kinder trinken? Hör dir die CD an und kreuze das richtige Getränk an.

Sally: ☐   ☐   Mark: ☐   ☐

Janet: ☐   ☐   Peter: ☐   ☐

Diana: ☐   ☐

b) Ergänze nun die Sätze.

1. Sally wants a _____.

   She doesn't want a glass of milk.

2. Mark wants _____.

   He doesn't _____.

3. Janet wants _____.

   She _____.

4. Peter _____.

   He _____.

5. Diana _____.

   She _____.

And you? What do you want to drink?

I want _____ . I don't want _____.

Das Verb want
I want = ich will   he/she wants = er/sie will
I don't want = ich will nicht   he/she doesn't want = er/sie will nicht

Unit 6: Food and drinks

Exercise 3

Kannst du diese Getränke erraten?

1. RETAW FO SSALG A   a glass of water
2. KLIM FO PUC A   _____
3. ECIUJ EGNARO FO ELTTOB A _____
4. AOCOC FO PUC A   _____
5. ECIUJ ELPPA FO ELTTOB A   _____
6. KLIM FO SSALG A   _____
7. AET FO PUC A   _____
8. KLIM FO ELTTOB A   _____
9. EEFFOC FO PUC A   _____

Exercise 4

a) Kreise alle Lebensmittel mit einem grünen Stift ein.
b) Kreise alle Getränke mit einem blauen Stift ein.

bananas   school   milk   peaches

potatoes   book   apple juice   ears   butter

chips   coffee   tomato   teacher

bathroom   peas   sister   strawberry   father

melon   oranges   grapes

cherries   water   cocoa   rubber

c) Wie viele Wörter bleiben übrig? _____

Test: Food and drinks

Exercise 1

Finde in diesem Suchrätsel zwölf Dinge, die man essen oder trinken kann, und trage sie dann in die richtige Tabellenspalte ein.

J	O	N	I	O	N	S	H	Y	Z
M	I	L	K	C	O	C	O	A	K
H	E	C	H	E	R	R	I	E	S
E	Q	K	C	O	F	F	E	E	K
S	I	Q	P	L	U	M	S	F	E
G	R	A	P	E	S	P	C	L	X
P	O	T	A	T	O	E	S	G	U
J	P	E	A	S	T	E	A	H	X
Q	Q	C	A	R	R	O	T	S	L
C	O	S	O	R	A	N	G	E	S

Food	Drinks

Unit 6: Food and drinks

Exercise 2

Hör dir die CD an und kreuze an, was Max und Pamela mögen.

Max: ☐ cherries ☐ melon ☐ plums ☐ peaches

☐ apple ice-cream ☐ orange ice-cream ☐ strawberry ice-cream

☐ carrots ☐ peas ☐ potatoes ☐ onions

☐ cocoa ☐ coffee ☐ milk ☐ apple juice

Pamela: ☐ peaches ☐ apples ☐ plums ☐ melon

☐ cherry ice-cream ☐ strawberry ice-cream ☐ banana ice-cream

☐ tomatoes ☐ carrots ☐ peas ☐ potatoes

☐ tea ☐ milk ☐ orange juice ☐ apple juice

Exercise 3

a) Hör dir die CD an und lies das Gedicht mit.

A nice cup of tea

I like a nice cup of tea in the morning
For to start the day you see
And at half-past eleven
Well my idea of Heaven
Is a nice cup of tea.

I like a nice cup of tea with my dinner
And a nice cup of tea with my tea
And when it's time for bed
There's a lot to be said
For a nice cup of tea.

b) Wie viele Tassen Tee trinkt diese Person am Tag? _____

Tipp: Du kannst die Frage zum Gedicht auch beantworten, wenn du nicht jedes Wort verstehst. Zähl einfach, wie oft a nice cup of tea im Gedicht vorkommt!

Unit 6: Food and drinks

Unit 7: Meals and shopping

A Meals

Exercise 1

Track 35

Hör dir die CD an und schreibe die Zahl vor das Wort, das du hörst.

- [ ] apple
- [ ] cheese sandwich
- [ ] crisps
- [ ] carrots
- [ ] chocolate bar
- [ ] biscuits
- [ ] ham roll
- [ ] a piece of cake
- [ ] muffin
- [ ] sweets

Exercise 2

Track 36

Welcher Pausensnack gehört welchem Kind? Hör dir die CD an und schreibe die richtigen Namen unter die Butterbrotdosen.

Exercise 3

Schreibe nun auf, was in jeder Frühstücksbox ist.

 Tipp: Wenn du nicht mehr genau weißt, wie man manche Wörter schreibt, sieh dir noch einmal die vorherigen Übungen an oder schau im Wörterverzeichnis nach!

Exercise 4

Wann isst oder trinkst du diese Dinge? Lies die Wörter und trage sie in den richtigen Kasten ein.

Breakfast (Frühstück)	Snack	Dinner (Mittagessen)

cornflakes   a glass of milk   a cheese roll
apple juice   fish and chips   a glass of water
a piece of cake   spaghetti   biscuits   green salad
toast with butter and jam   bread   an egg   chicken

Unit 7: Meals and shopping

Exercise 5

Hör die die CD an und ergänze die Geschichte mit den Wörtern im Kasten.

eggs   milk   cornflakes   water
cherry   peas   melon   jam

A funny boy

Peter is a funny boy. His favourite food is cold pizza and _____ for breakfast.

His snack at school is always a cheese and _____ sandwich.

He always drinks _____ . He never drinks _____ .

His favourite cake is strawberry or _____ . He never eats _____ or grapes. For dinner he always eats _____ , fish and chips. He never eats carrots or _____ . He really is a funny boy.

> always = immer
> never = nie
>
> **always** und **never** stehen meist direkt vor dem Verb:
> He **always** drinks water.
> He **never** eats carrots.

Exercise 6

Und du? Was isst oder trinkst du immer (jeden Tag), was nie?

I always eat _____ .

I never eat _____ .

I always drink _____ .

I never drink _____ .

_____ .

_____ .

Unit 7: Meals and shopping

Exercise 7

Schau dir das Bild an. Lies dann die Sätze und schreibe **yes** (ja) oder **no** (nein) dahinter.

1. The mother is eating an apple. _yes_
2. The father is eating cornflakes. _no_
3. The boy is eating cornflakes. ____
4. The mother is drinking a cup of coffee. ____
5. The father is eating toast. ____
6. The girl is eating toast. ____
7. The father is drinking a cup of tea. ____
8. The girl has a banana for school. ____
9. The boy has apple juice for school. ____
10. The cat is drinking milk. ____

Unit 7: Meals and shopping

B Shopping

Exercise 1

Du willst fürs Frühstück einkaufen und ihr habt **nichts** mehr im Haus. Erstelle eine Einkaufsliste.

Exercise 2

Track 38

Hör dir die CD an und ergänze die Einkaufsliste.

*newspaper = Zeitung

Unit 7: Meals and shopping

Exercise 3

Dieses Spiel kannst du allein oder mit jemandem zusammen spielen. Stell einen Spielstein auf das Startfeld. Mit einem Würfel wird bestimmt, wie viele Felder du vorrücken darfst. Wenn du auf einem Feld mit einer Leiter landest, darfst du nach oben gehen. Wenn du auf einer Schlange landest, rutschst du wieder nach unten. Wenn du auf einem Feld mit einem englischen Wort landest und dieses Wort auf Deutsch sagen kannst, bekommst du 5 Punkte.

Snakes and ladders

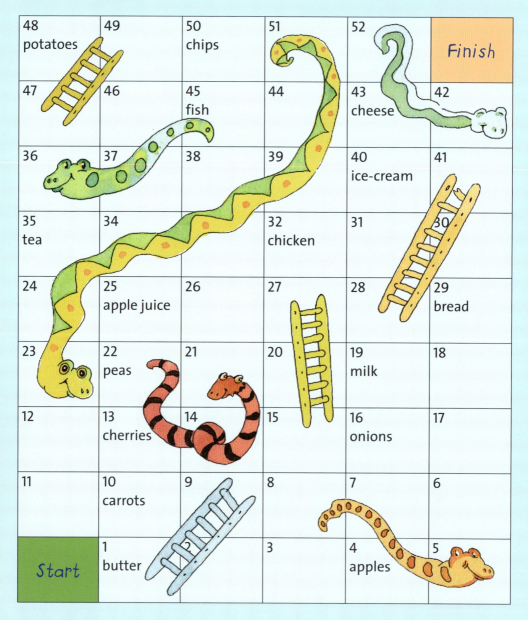

Unit 7: Meals and shopping

Exercise 4

Löse dieses Kreuzworträtsel.
Trage alle Begriffe auf Englisch ein.

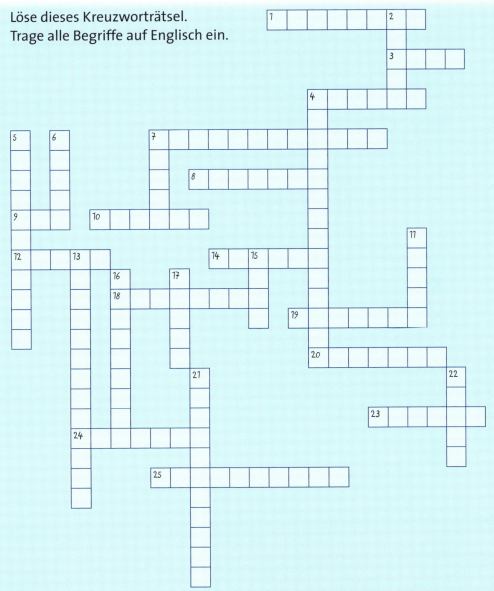

Across →:
1 Eiscreme **3** Erbsen **4** Kaffee **7** Schokoriegel **8** Karotten **9** Tee
10 Chips **12** Saft **14** Muffin **18** Kartoffeln **19** Keks **20** Schinkenbrötchen
23 Bonbons **24** Hähnchen **25** grüner Salat

Down ↓:
2 Apfel **4** Käsesandwich **5** Tomatensaft **6** Pizza **7** Pommes frites
11 Frucht, Obst **13** Schokoladenkuchen **15** Fisch **16** Spaghetti **17** Salat
21 Orangensaft **22** Wasser

Unit 7: Meals and shopping

Test: Meals and shopping

Exercise 1

Ordne diese Wörter in drei Gruppen ein: Hauptgericht = rotes Kästchen, Getränke = blaues Kästchen, Nachtisch = grünes Kästchen.

- ☐ apple juice
- ☐ chicken
- ☐ fish
- ☐ orange juice
- ☐ potatoes
- ☐ spaghetti

- ☐ carrots
- ☐ chips
- ☐ fruit salad
- ☐ peas
- ☐ tomato juice
- ☐ tea

- ☐ coffee
- ☐ cocoa
- ☐ ice-cream
- ☐ pizza
- ☐ green salad
- ☐ water

Exercise 2

Setze die fehlenden Vokale ein.

D _ NN _ R

_ C _ - CR _ _ M

M _ LK

F _ SH

CH _ CK _ N

CH _ C _ L _ T _

SN _ CK

T _ M _ T _

P _ T _ T _ _ S

BR _ _ KF _ ST

CH _ _ S _

_ GGS

_ PPL _ J _ _ C _

C _ K _

P _ ZZ _

S _ L _ D

Wie viele Vokale hast du gebraucht?

Unit 7: Meals and shopping

Exercise 3

Track 39

Wer bestellt was?
Hör dir die CD an und verbinde die Namen mit den Kuchen und Getränken.

	glass of apple juice
	chocolate cake
Mr Brown	strawberry cake
Betty	pizza
David	cup of coffee
John	glass of milk
	cup of cocoa
	apple cake

Exercise 4

Streiche immer das Wort durch, das nicht zu den beiden anderen passt.

1.	breakfast	cheese	dinner
2.	chocolate cake	biscuit	fish
3.	apple juice	pizza	tea
4.	newspaper	bread	butter
5.	ice-cream	chicken	spaghetti
6.	coffee	cup	glass

Unit 7: Meals and shopping   77

Unit 8: In town

A In the street

Exercise 1

Track 40

Hör dir die CD an und verbinde die Wörter mit den Fahrzeugen.

1

2

3

4

5

a black taxi

a brown lorry

an orange car

a green bus

a pink tram

a blue motorbike

a red fire engine

a black train

a yellow bike

a white ambulance

6

7

8

9

10

Exercise 2

Track 41

a) Hör dir die CD an und male die Fahrzeuge in der richtigen Farbe aus. Lege diese Farben bereit: red, blue, orange, green, black, pink, brown, yellow.

b) Schreibe dann unter jedes Bild einen Satz.

The taxi is yellow.

Unit 8: In town

Exercise 3

Trage die englischen Wörter ein.

In the street

Unit 8: In town

Exercise 4

a) Schau dir das Bild auf S. 80 noch einmal an und beantworte die Fragen.

1. Can you see two fire engines?   No, I can't.
2. Can you see one fire engine?   Yes, I can.
3. Can you see a train?   _____
4. Can you see a lorry?   _____
5. Can you see five cars?   _____
6. Can you see a girl on a bike?   _____
7. Can you see two bikes?   _____

b) Schreibe nun fünf Sätze über das Bild.

I can see a fire engine.
I can see _____.
I can see _____.
_____.
_____.
_____.

Wenn du beschreiben möchtest, was du auf einem Bild siehst, beginnst du deine Sätze mit: I can see …

Unit 8: In town   81

B   Places in town

Exercise 1

Finde heraus, wie diese Gebäude und Orte auf Englisch heißen. Die Tabelle unten auf der Seite hilft dir, den Code zu entschlüsseln!

2, 6, 9, 4, 7, 8
1   cinema

16, 1, 24, 20, 1, 19, 19, 6, 2, 4
2   _____

11, 6, 5, 10, 8, 10, 21
3   _____

24, 2, 18, 1, 1, 11
4   _____

2, 18, 3, 10, 2, 18
5   _____

7, 3, 24, 4, 3, 7
6   _____

20, 1, 21   24, 18, 1, 16
7   _____

16, 4, 20   24, 18, 1, 16
8   _____

16, 11, 8, 21, 12, 10, 1, 3, 9, 13
9   _____

24, 3, 16, 4, 10, 7, 8, 10, 22, 4, 20
10   _____

5, 6, 22, 4   24, 18, 1, 16
11   _____

18, 1, 24, 16, 6, 20, 8, 11
12   _____

A	B	C	D	E	F	G	H	I	J	K	L	M	N	O	P	Q	R	S	T	U	V	W	X	Y	Z
8	5	2	13	4	19	12	18	6	15	22	11	7	9	1	16	25	10	24	20	3	23	26	14	21	17

Exercise 2

Track 42

Hör dir die CD an und schreibe die Zahl vor das Wort, das du hörst.

- ☐ cinema
- ☐ playground
- ☐ school
- ☐ church
- ☐ library
- ☐ supermarket
- ☐ museum
- ☐ toy shop
- ☐ post office
- ☐ hospital

> Wenn du jemandem vorschlagen möchtest, irgendwohin zu gehen, sagst du: Let's go …, z. B. **Let's go** to the library. Lass uns zur Bücherei gehen.

Exercise 3

a) Ergänze die Sätze.

1. Ann: Let's go to the _____.

2. Bill: Let's go to the _____.

3. Tim: Let's go to the _____.

4. Mary: Let's go to the _____.

5. Barbara: Let's go to the _____.

b) Schreibe nun in ganzen Sätzen, wohin die Kinder gehen wollen.

<u>Ann wants to go to the cinema.</u>

Bill wants to go _____.

Tim _____.

Mary _____.

Barbara _____.

Unit 8: In town

he/she wants to = er/sie will
he/she must = er/sie muss

Exercise 4

Schau dir die Einkaufslisten von Jack und Jill an. In welche Geschäfte müssen sie gehen?

Jack's shopping list

apples
flowers
book
cat food

Jill's shopping list

eggs
yoyo
bike
shoes

1. Jack wants to buy apples. **He must go to the supermarket.**
2. He wants to buy flowers. He must go to the _____.
3. He wants to buy a book. He must _____.
4. He wants to buy cat food. _____.
5. Jill wants to buy eggs. She must go to the _____.
6. She wants to buy a yoyo. She must _____.
7. She wants to buy a bike. _____.
8. She wants to buy shoes. _____.
9. And now she wants to play. She wants to go to the _____!

Tipp: Die Namen der Geschäfte für die Sätze 2, 3 und 8 kennst du vielleicht noch nicht, du kannst sie aber ganz leicht erraten. Versuch's einfach mal!

Exercise 5

Track 43

a) Hör dir die CD an und zeichne Jacks Weg in die Skizze ein. An der Bushaltestelle geht's los!

b) Schreibe nun alle Orte in der richtigen Reihenfolge auf:

1. bus stop
2. _____
3. _____
4. _____
5. _____
6. _____
7. _____
8. _____
9. bus stop

Unit 8: In town

Test: In town

Exercise 1

Lies die Geschichte und trage die fehlenden Wörter ein.

Next week it is Henry's birthday. His mother, Mrs Brown, wants to buy a

goldfish for Henry. So she goes to the  _pet shop_ . Then she

goes to the  _____ for a new game of Monopoly.

She sees her friend, Mark. He is in front of the _____

_____ . He has got a yellow  _____ . In the street

there are a lot of vehicles*. First there is a big brown _____ ,

then behind it there is an orange _____ ,

a black  _____ and a pink _____ .

There is a _____

and an  _____

next to the _____ .

*vehicles = Fahrzeuge

Unit 8: In town

Exercise 2

Löse dieses Kreuzworträtsel. Trage alle Begriffe auf Englisch ein.

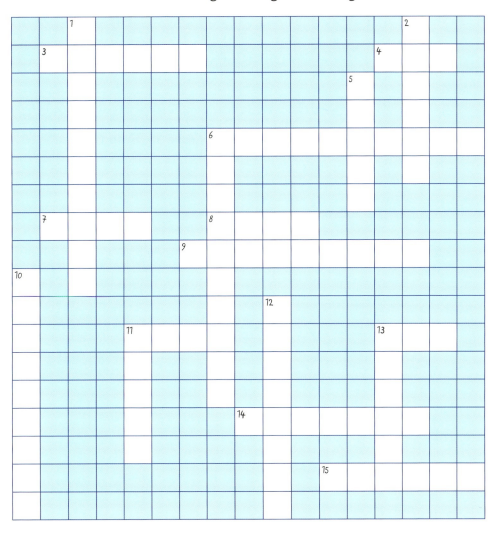

Across → :
3 Kino   **4** Bus   **6** Spielplatz   **7** Fahrrad   **8** Straßenbahn   **9** Motorrad
11 Taxi   **13** Auto   **14** Bücherei   **15** Schule

Down ↓ :
1 Feuerwehrauto   **2** Museum   **5** Lastwagen   **6** Postamt   **10** Krankenwagen
11 Eisenbahn   **12** Krankenhaus   **13** Kirche

Unit 9: Animals

A On a farm

Exercise 1

Track 44

a) Welche dieser Tiere kennst du schon? Schreibe die Wörter unter die Bilder.
b) Hör dir nun die CD an und ergänze die fehlenden Wörter.

Farm animals

cow   pig   horse   goat   sheep   cock
lamb   duck   chicken   turkey

Exercise 2

Verbinde die Wörter mit den Zahlen.

1	three
2	six
3	two
4	eight
5	one
6	four
7	nine
8	seven
9	five

Exercise 3

Zähle nun die Tiere und schreibe Sätze. Schreibe die Zahlen dabei aus.

1. There is _one horse_ _____ on the farm.
2. There are _____ on the farm.
3. _____ on the farm.
4. _____ on the farm.
5. _____ on the farm.
6. _____ on the farm.
7. _____ on the farm.
8. _____ on the farm.
9. _____ on the farm.
10. _____ on the farm.

Erinnerst du dich?
Du schreibst there is, wenn das Nomen in der Einzahl steht.
Du schreibst there are, wenn das Nomen in der Mehrzahl steht.

Exercise 4

Tracks 45/46

a) Welches Tier gehört auf welche Weide? Hör dir die CD an und trage jedes Tier in die richtige Weide ein.

cow   pig   horse   goat   sheep   cock
lamb   duck   hen   turkey

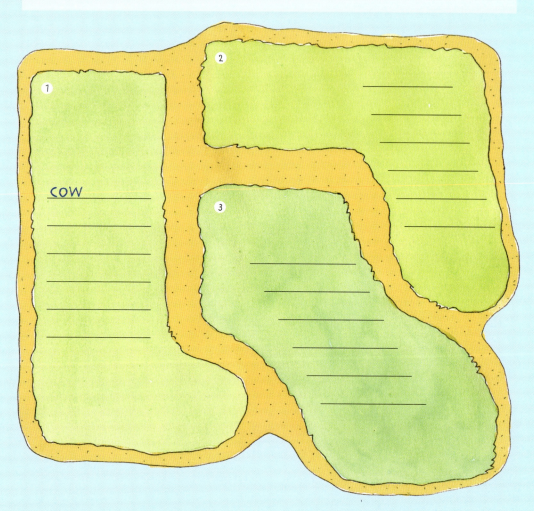

b) Hör dir nun wieder die CD an und beantworte die Fragen.
Beispiel:
Der Sprecher auf der CD fragt: Where is the **cow**?
Du sagst: The **cow** is in field number **one**.

where is? = wo ist?

Unit 9: Animals

Exercise 5

Löse das Kreuzworträtsel. Trage die englischen Wörter ein.

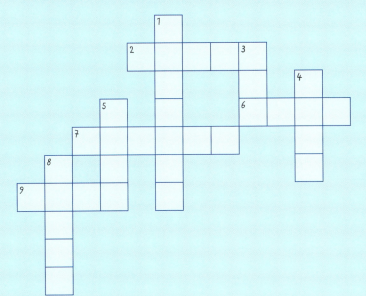

Across →:
2 Schaf
6 Ziege
7 Truthahn
9 Hahn

Down ↓:
1 Huhn
3 Schwein
4 Lamm
5 Ente
8 Pferd

Exercise 6

Wer bin ich? Lies die Sätze und rate, welches Tier das ist.

1. I am big. You can ride on me. I am a _horse_ .
2. I am big. I give you milk. I am a _____ .
3. I am not big. I give you eggs. I can't swim. I am a _____ .
4. I am not big and not small. I give you wool. I am a _____ .
5. I am not big and not small. People think that I am dirty but I am not! I am a _____ .
6. I am small. I give you eggs. I can swim. I am a _____ .
7. My mother is number 4. I am a _____ .

In dieser Übung kommen neue Wörter vor: ride, wool und dirty. Kennst du sie? Wenn nicht, dann sieh im Wörterverzeichnis nach!

Unit 9: Animals

B At the zoo

Exercise 1
Wie heißen diese Zootiere auf Englisch? Schwierige Wörter kannst du – wie immer – im Wörterverzeichnis nachschlagen.

monkey

koala bear

hippo

sea lion

tiger

kangaroo

penguin

lion

elephant

giraffe

rhino

crocodile

Unit 9: Animals

Exercise 2

Track 47

Hör dir die CD an und schreibe die Zahl vor das Wort, das du hörst.

- ☐ monkey
- ☐ sea lion
- ☐ penguin
- ☐ giraffe
- ☐ koala bear
- ☐ tiger
- ☐ lion
- ☐ rhino
- ☐ hippo
- ☐ kangaroo
- ☐ elephant
- ☐ crocodile

Exercise 3

Track 48

a) Welches Tier mögen diese Kinder? Hör dir die CD an und kreuze das richtige Tier an.

Jenny: ☐ ☐   Jack: ☐ ☐

Pamela: ☐ ☐   Peter: ☐ ☐

Ann: ☐ ☐

Erinnerst du dich?
he/she likes = er/sie mag
he/she doesn't like = er/sie mag nicht

Unit 9: Animals

b) Ergänze nun die Sätze.

1. Jenny likes _tigers_ . She doesn't like _giraffes_ .
2. Jack likes _____ . He doesn't like _____ .
3. Pamela _____
   _____ .
4. Peter _____
   _____ .
5. Ann _____
   _____ .

And you?

I like _____ . I don't like _____ .

Exercise 4

Track 49

a) Hör dir die CD an. Lies dann die Sätze und kreuze an, ob sie richtig **(right)** oder falsch **(wrong)** sind.

		right	wrong
1.	Pam and her father are at the zoo.	☐	☐
2.	Pam wants to see the elephants.	☐	☐
3.	There are four monkeys.	☐	☐
4.	There are three baby monkeys.	☐	☐
5.	The mother has a banana.	☐	☐
6.	The monkey with the banana is under the table.	☐	☐
7.	The father monkey is in a basket in the tree.	☐	☐

Unit 9: Animals

b) Hör dir die CD noch einmal an und male alle Personen und Affen, die erwähnt werden, an die richtige Stelle.

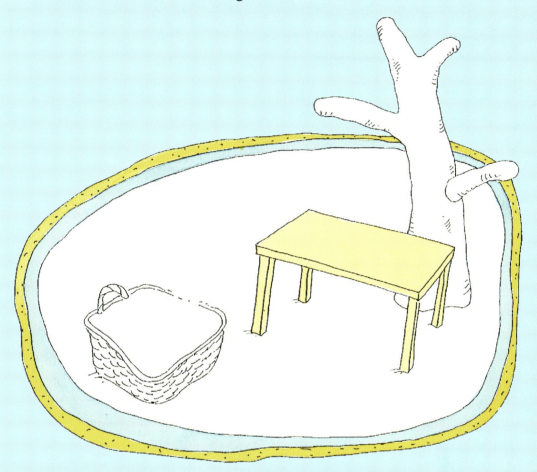

c) Vervollständige nun die Sätze:

Pam and her _____ are at the zoo.

Pam wants to see the _____ .

There are _____ monkeys, a father, a mother and _____ baby monkeys.

One _____ has a banana. He is under the table with the _____ .

The baby monkey with no banana is on the _____ .

The _____ monkey is in the tree. And the _____ monkey is in a basket next to the table.

Test: Animals

 Exercise 1

Ergänze die fehlenden Vokale.

1. G ___ ___ T
2. S ___ ___ L ___ ___ N
3. M ___ N K ___ ___
4. K ___ N G ___ R ___ ___
5. T ___ R K ___ ___

 Exercise 2

1. This animal is _a tiger and a sheep_____.
2. This animal is_____.
3. _____.

Exercise 3

a) Trenne die Wörter mit einem Bleistift. Unterstreiche dann alle Zootiere blau, alle anderen Tiere rot.

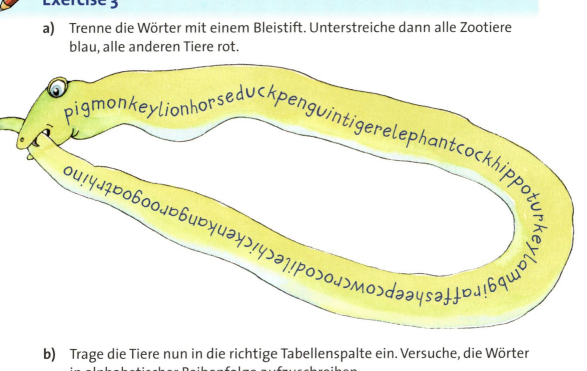

b) Trage die Tiere nun in die richtige Tabellenspalte ein. Versuche, die Wörter in alphabetischer Reihenfolge aufzuschreiben.

Zoo animals	Farm animals

Unit 9: Animals

Unit 10: Celebrations

A   Seasonal holidays

Exercise 1

Track 50

a) Schau dir das Bild an und trage alle Wörter ein, die du schon kennst.

> Christmas tree   candles   stars   bells
> chocolate   angel   presents   Christmas cards
> nuts   Christmas biscuits

Christmas

b) Hör dir nun die CD an und ergänze den Text.

We have a big _____ at Christmas. On the tree there are _____ and _____ . There are _____ and a lot of _____ . And there is an _____ at the top. Under the tree there are a lot of _____ with ribbons on them. We get lots of _____ . We have _____ and we always have lots of _____ .

Exercise 2

a) Entschlüssle die Wörter auf der Karte mithilfe der Tabelle und schreibe den Satz auf.

A	B	C	D	E	F	G	H	I	J	K	L	M
Z	Y	X	W	V	U	T	S	R	Q	P	O	N

N	O	P	Q	R	S	T	U	V	W	X	Y	Z
M	L	K	J	I	H	G	F	E	D	C	B	A

C _ _ _ _ _ _ _ _   _ N _

_ _ _ _ _ _ _   _ _ _

_ _ _ _ _   P _ _ _ _ _ _ _ _

_ _   _ _ _

25th _ _   D _ _ _ _ _ _ _ _ .

b) Was bedeutet der Satz auf Deutsch? Unterstreiche die richtige Lösung.

1. Kinder in England bekommen ihre Geschenke am 25. Dezember.
2. Kinder in Großbritannien bekommen ihre Geschenke am 25. Dezember.
3. Kinder in Großbritannien bekommen ihre Geschenke am 24. Dezember.

Exercise 3

The Easter rabbit was here. Where are the eggs?

a) Der Osterhase war hier. Wo sind die Eier? Ergänze die Sätze.

1. The purple egg is _____.
2. The yellow egg _____.
3. The red _____.
4. The _____.

 in = in   on = auf   behind = hinter   under = unter

b) Jetzt bist du der Osterhase. Lies die Sätze und male die Eier an die richtigen Stellen im Bild.
   1. The orange egg is under the table.
   2. The brown egg is in the bookshelf.
   3. The pink egg is on the chair.

Exercise 4

Track 51

Halloween

ghost   witch   spider   bat   cat

a) Hör dir die CD an und trage die richtige Zahl ein.

There are _____ cats.

There are _____ spiders.

There are _____ ghosts.

There are _____ witches.

There are _____ bats.

b) Schreibe nun die richtigen Wörter unter die Figuren. Du kannst das Bild dann ausmalen, wenn du möchtest.

Unit 10: Celebrations

B   My birthday

Exercise 1

Track 52

a) Zähle die Kerzen auf den Geburtstagstorten und ergänze die Sätze.

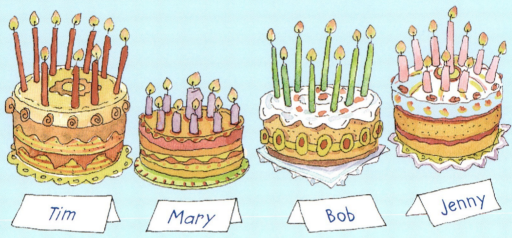

1. Mary is _____ years old today.
2. Happy birthday, Jenny! You are _____ years old today.
3. It is Bob's birthday today. He is _____ years old today.
4. And Tim is _____ years old today. Happy birthday, Tim.

b) Hör dir nun die CD an und zeichne die Kerzen auf die Torten von John, Susan und Paul.

Unit 10: Celebrations

Exercise 2

Tracks 53/54

Linda's birthday calendar

JANUARY	FEBRUARY	MARCH
		Alex
APRIL	MAY	JUNE
JULY	AUGUST	SEPTEMBER
OCTOBER	NOVEMBER	DECEMBER

Janet, Tom, Linda, Dad, Mum, Robert, Tim, Sally, Susan

a) Hör dir die CD an und zeige auf den richtigen Monat.
b) Hör dir nun an, was Linda und Tom sagen, und trage die Namen in den Geburtstagskalender ein.
c) In welchen beiden Monaten hat niemand Geburtstag?

_____ and _____

Unit 10: Celebrations

Exercise 3

Wann haben die Kinder Geburtstag? Schau dir noch einmal Lindas Geburts-tagskalender an und vervollständige die Sätze.

1. Robert's birthday is in _January_ .
2. Tim's birthday is in _____ .
3. Susan's birthday is in _____ .
4. Alex's birthday is in _____ .
5. _____ birthday is in July.
6. _____ birthday is in April.
7. _____ birthday is in May.
8. _____ birthday is in _____ .

 Denk an den Apostroph vor dem -s!
Tims Geburtstag = Tim's birthday
Susans Geburtstag = Susan's birthday

 ### Exercise 4

When's your birthday? In welchem Monat hast du Geburtstag?

My birthday is in _____ .

Exercise 5

Beantworte die Fragen.

1. When's your mother's birthday? It's in _____ .
2. When's your father's birthday? It's in _____ .
3. When's your best friend's birthday? It's in _____ .

Exercise 6

Ergänze in diesem Geburtstagskalender zunächst die Monate auf Englisch. Trage dann alle deine Freunde und Verwandten ein.

My birthday calendar

Test: Celebrations

Exercise 1

In diesem Suchrätsel haben sich 15 Wörter zu den Themen Weihnachten, Ostern und Halloween versteckt. Umkreise sie und trage sie dann in die richtige Tabellenspalte ein.

P	Z	X	F	C	A	N	D	L	E	S	S
Z	G	G	H	O	S	T	S	N	C	Z	R
A	O	C	C	U	T	R	E	E	H	B	H
J	H	Y	Z	S	P	I	D	E	R	S	K
H	E	C	A	T	S	E	S	T	A	R	S
Q	K	N	U	T	S	E	G	G	S	K	S
I	W	I	T	C	H	E	S	Q	F	E	P
C	L	X	G	U	J	A	N	G	E	L	H
X	Q	P	R	E	S	E	N	T	S	Q	L
C	O	S	X	R	A	B	B	I	T	V	A
C	A	R	D	S	C	O	U	I	C	A	O
X	L	B	E	L	L	S	B	A	T	S	R

Christmas	Easter	Halloween

Exercise 2

Easter, Halloween or Christmas? Lies die Sätze und trage auf Englisch ein, um welches Fest es sich handelt.

1. You have a big tree. That is at _Christmas_____.
2. You can be a ghost or a witch. That is at _____.
3. You can find eggs. That is at _____.
4. You have a lot of candles. That is at _____.
5. You get presents. That is at _____.
6. You can sometimes see a very big "rabbit". That is at _____.
7. You can see bats and spiders. That is at _____.

Exercise 3

a) Ergänze die fehlenden Buchstaben.

1. JAN _ _ RY
2. J _ _ E
3. AP _ _ L
4. M _ _
5. D _ _ _ _ _ R
6. J _ _ Y
7. FEB _ _ _ _ _
8. M _ _ _ H
9. O _ _ _ _ _ R
10. S _ P _ _ _ _ R
11. A _ G _ _ T
12. N _ _ _ _ ER

b) Schreibe die Monate nun in der richtigen Reihenfolge.

1. _____
2. _____
3. _____
4. _____
5. _____
6. _____
7. _____
8. _____
9. _____
10. _____
11. _____
12. _____

Unit 10: Celebrations

Wörterverzeichnis

A
a lot of – viele
alarm clock – Wecker
always – immer
ambulance – Krankenwagen
angel – Engel
animal – Tier
apple – Apfel
apple juice – Apfelsaft
aquarium – Aquarium
attic – Dachboden
aunt – Tante

B
ballet – Ballett
banana – Banane
basket – Korb
bat – Fledermaus
bathroom – Badezimmer
be – sein
bed – Bett
bedroom – Schlafzimmer
bedside table – Nachttisch
behind – hinter
bell – Glocke
big – groß
bike – Fahrrad
bike shop – Fahrradladen
birthday – Geburtstag
biscuit – Keks
black – schwarz
blanket – Decke
blue – blau
board – Tafel
book – Buch
bookshelf – Regal
bottle – Flasche
boy – Junge
bread – Brot
breakfast – Frühstück
Britain – Großbritannien
brother – Bruder
brown – braun
bus – Bus
bus stop – Bushaltestelle
butter – Butter

C
cage – Käfig
cake – Kuchen
calendar – Kalender
can – können
candle – Kerze
cap – Kappe
car – Auto
card – Karte
carpet – Teppich
carrot – Möhre, Karotte
CD-player – CD-Spieler
celebration – Fest, Feier
chair – Stuhl
chalk – Kreide
cheese – Käse
cherry – Kirsche
chess – Schach
chicken – Hähnchen
chicken – Huhn
chips – Pommes frites
chocolate bar – Schokoriegel
Christmas – Weihnachten
church – Kirche
cinema – Kino
classroom – Klassenzimmer
cock – Hahn

cocoa – Kakao
coffee – Kaffee
computer – Computer
cornflakes – Cornflakes
cousin – Cousin, Kusine
cow – Kuh
crisps – Chips
crocodile – Krokodil
cup – Tasse
cycling – Radfahren

D
dark – dunkel
day – Tag
dining room – Esszimmer
dinner – Mittagessen
dirty – schmutzig
dog – Hund
dominoes – Domino
door – Tür
drink – Getränk
drink – trinken
duck – Ente
duster – Tafellappen

E
ear – Ohr
Easter – Ostern
eat – essen
egg – Ei
elephant – Elefant
England – England
English book – Englischbuch
exercise book – Heft
eye – Auge

F
farm – Bauernhof
father – Vater
felt-pen – Filzstift
find – finden

fire engine – Feuerwehrauto
flower – Blume
foot, feet – Fuß, Füße
football – Fußball
freckles – Sommersprossen
friend – Freund/in
fruit – Frucht, Obst
funny – komisch

G
game – Spiel
German book – Deutschbuch
get – bekommen
ghost – Gespenst
giraffe – Giraffe
girl – Mädchen
glass – Glas
glasses – Brille
go – gehen
goat – Ziege
goldfish – Goldfisch
grandfather – Großvater
grandmother – Großmutter
grapes – Weintrauben
green – grün
guitar – Gitarre

H
hair – Haare
hall – Flur
ham – Schinken
hamster – Hamster
hand – Hand
have – haben
head – Kopf
heaven – Himmel
help – helfen
hen – Henne
her – ihr, ihre
hippo – Flusspferd
his – sein, seine

hockey – Hockey
homework – Hausaufgaben
horse – Pferd
horse riding – Reiten
hospital – Krankenhaus
house – Haus

I
ice skating – Eislaufen
ice-cream – Eiscreme
in – in
ink cartridge – Tintenpatrone
inline skating – Inlineskating

J
jacket – Jacke
jam – Marmelade
judo – Judo
juice – Saft

K
kangaroo – Känguru
kitchen – Küche
kiwi – Kiwi
koala bear – Koala

L
ladder – Leiter
lamb – Lamm
lamp – Lampe
library – Bücherei
like – mögen
lion – Löwe
live – leben, wohnen
living room – Wohnzimmer
long – lang
look for – suchen
lorry – Lastwagen
love – lieben

M
map – Landkarte
maths book – Mathebuch
melon – Melone
milk – Milch
mobile phone – Handy
monkey – Affe
morning – Morgen
mother – Mutter
motorbike – Motorrad
mouse – Maus
mouth – Mund
muffin – Muffin
museum – Museum
music – Musik
must – müssen

N
name – Name
never – nie
newspaper – Zeitung
next to – neben
nice – schön, nett
nose – Nase
nut – Nuss

O
old – alt
on – auf
onion – Zwiebel
orange – orange
orange – Orange
orange juice – Orangensaft

P
pea – Erbse
peach – Pfirsich
pen – Füller, Stift
pencil – Bleistift, Buntstift
pencil case – Etui
pencil sharpener – Bleistiftspitzer

penguin – Pinguin
pet shop – Tierhandlung
piece – Stück
pig – Schwein
pink – rosa
play – spielen
playground – Spielplatz
plum – Pflaume
post office – Postamt
potato – Kartoffel
present – Geschenk
pullover – Pullover
purple – lila
put on – anziehen

R
rabbit – Kaninchen, Hase
red – rot
rhino – Nashorn
ribbon – Band
ride – reiten
roll – Brötchen
room – Zimmer
rubber – Radiergummi
ruler – Lineal

S
salad – Salat
sandwich – Sandwich
school – Schule
schoolbag – Schultasche
sea lion – Seelöwe
sheep – Schaf
shoe – Schuh
shop – Laden, Geschäft
shopping list – Einkaufsliste
short – kurz
sister – Schwester
sleep – schlafen
small – klein
snake – Schlange

sometimes – manchmal
spider – Spinne
sponge – Schwamm
stamp – stampfen
star – Stern
strawberry – Erdbeere
street – Straße
supermarket – Supermarkt
sweets – Bonbons
swim – schwimmen
swimming – Schwimmen

T
table – Tisch
table tennis – Tischtennis
taxi – Taxi
tea – Tee
teacher – Lehrer/in
tennis – Tennis
tennis racket – Tennisschläger
tiger – Tiger
time – Zeit
toast – Toastbrot
toe – Zehe
tomato – Tomate
town – Stadt
toy shop – Spielzeugladen
train – Eisenbahn
tram – Straßenbahn
tree – Baum
turkey – Truthahn
TV – Fernseher

U
uncle – Onkel
under – unter

W
vegetable – Gemüse
vehicle – Fahrzeug

Wörterverzeichnis

X
want – wollen
wardrobe – Kleiderschrank
wash – waschen
watch TV – fernsehen
wear – tragen
where – wo
white – weiß
wiggle – wackeln
window – Fenster
witch – Hexe
wool – Wolle

Y
year – Jahr
yellow – gelb
yoyo – Jojo

Z
zoo – Zoo